For Faith

still
teaching me
what it means
to be married
after sixty-two years

I Do:

Quotations on Marriage, from the Married, the Unmarried and Me

A selection of quotes as they apply to marriage.

Published by Carl Scovel

ISBN 978-1-7351886-1-4
Library of Congress Control Number: 2020910644

Printed in the United States of America

I DO tells the story of marriage as described in short quotations from more than two hundred men and women, beginning with Homer in 850 BCE and concluding with Michelle Obama in 2020.

The story of marriage is filled with affection, passion, frustration, fulfillment, boredom, betrayal, sacrifice, service, learning, leaving, loyalty, and love. As a husband, father, grandfather, and minister who has presided at more than six hundred weddings, I've been fascinated by the varieties, enigmas, and surprises in the marriages I've observed. That's probably why I began to collect quotations about marriage thirty years ago. I've organized these into a narrative that begins with someone contemplating marriage and ends with the solitude of the survivor.

I put these together thinking of the brides and grooms whom I've known and their families, friends, and offspring. I was thinking also of cohabiting couples, singles thinking of marriage, children wondering why their parents got married and anyone interested in the delights and dangers of connubial life. People like these might be my readers.

A word on what you are about to read. All but a few of the contributors' names have been changed. Quotations appear in bold typeface, my commentary in roman. As you read, remember that behind each of these quotes lies the experience of someone who has lived the challenges, questions, and blessings of a partnered relationship.

So here it is — a guide for the young, a companion for the middle-aged, and a source of memories for the elderly. Good reading to you all, and, I hope, a few smiles as well.

Carl Scovel

CONTENTS

Anyone who thinks being single is fun should try it on a Sunday afternoon.

Why Do We Marry?

We marry for many reasons: love, lust, hopes for happiness, ambition, fulfillment, financial advantage, family pressure, and loneliness. The last reason is one we find in the Bible, when God in Genesis 2:18 says, "It is not good for the earthling to be alone."

You may not have been told this before, but the first human in that ancient story was not a man, but an earthling, a creature whom God shaped from the soil, a creature without sexual identity. Seeing that this earthling was lonely, God put it to sleep, took a rib from its side and from that rib created a woman. The earthling then woke to discover that he was no longer an it, but a male. And right beside him — what a nice surprise! — was a female.

Here were two beings who complemented each other — man and woman, husband and wife, the founders of humanity and partners in the great scheme of creation.

Although it was the custom in ancient days for brides to move to their husband's home and live under the rule of their mother-in-law, Genesis challenges this custom. In 2:24 we read, "Therefore, a man shall leave his father and mother, and cling to his wife, and they shall become one flesh." This means that a husband's loyalty to his wife precedes his loyalty to his parents. That verse sets the gold standard for a good marriage, as we see in the following passage from the Talmud.

Woman was made
from the rib of man,
not from his head to
stand above him, nor from his
foot to stand beneath him,
but from his rib
to stand beside him.

THE TALMUD

Shakespeare, Ecclesiastes and a young bachelor in 1960 echo this viewpoint.

He is the half part of a blessed man
left to be finished by such as she;
and she a fair divided excellence
whose fullness of perfection lies in him.

KING JOHN, ACT 2, SCENE 1, WILLIAM SHAKESPEARE (1564–1616)

+++

Two are better than one ... for if they fall, one will lift up the other ... if two lie down together, they will keep each other warm.

ECCLESIASTES 4: 9–1

+++

Anyone who thinks that being single is fun should try it on Sunday afternoon.

+++

Why do we marry? We need company. In fact, humanity *needs* that we need company. Out of our need for company comes community, and out of community comes life, and life ensures that our humankind shall continue.

Marriage is a dance because both parties must move in common rhythm.

What is Marriage?

**An institution ordained for the mutual help
of husband and wife,
for the increase of mankind …
and the prevention of uncleanness.**

THE SAVOY DECLARATION OF 1658

+++

A job
A koan
A three-ring circus
An honorable estate

+++

Our last and best chance to grow up

JOSEPH BARTH
MINISTER OF KING'S CHAPEL (1955–1965)

+++

**An ecclesiola in ecclesia, that is,
a little church within the church.**

MARTIN LUTHER (1483–1546)

Not everyone thinks marriage is a great idea.

The only adventure open to the timid.

FRANÇOIS VOLTAIRE (1694–1778)

+++

**Bigamy is having one husband too many.
Monogamy is the same.**

ERICA JONG (1942–)

+++

A community consisting of one master, one mistress, and two slaves, making in all two.

AMBROSE BIERCE (1842–1914)
THE DEVIL'S DICTIONARY

+++

Here is one more metaphor for marriage. It's a dance. The old song says, *"It takes two to tango."* T. S. Eliot's ancestor, Thomas Elyot, put it more elegantly:

The association of man and woman in dancing, signifying matrimony — a dignified and commodious sacrament, two and two, a necessary conjunction, holding each other by the hand or arm which betokens concord.

THE BOOK OF THE GOVERNOR BY THOMAS ELYOT. 1531

Marriage is a dance because both parties must move in common rhythm in order to perform the daily rituals of washing, sweeping, cooking, phoning, shopping, talking, listening, making decisions, making money, making love, and raising children. To do all this and more the two must move in time to a music that sometimes only they can hear.

+++

The answer to the question, what is marriage, changed somewhat in the United States in 2003 when The Massachusetts Supreme Judicial Court ruled that to bar an individual "from the protection, benefits, and obligations of civil marriage solely because that person would marry a person of the same sex would violate the Massachusetts Constitution." The Court said that the longstanding prohibition against same sex marriage did not meet the rational test for either due process or equal protection. Other states followed suit and in 2015 the U.S. Supreme Court made this the law of the land. Although most church weddings are also civil weddings, this law does not obligate churches that oppose same sex marriages to conduct them.

It is not your love
that sustains your marriage,
but your marriage
that sustains your love.

What is Marriage Like?

It all depends on whom you ask, as we see in the following quotes.

It takes years to marry completely.
A happy wedlock is a long falling in love.
Men and women marry fractionally,
now a small fraction, then a large …
A complete marriage needs a long summer to ripen in
and a long winter to mellow and season in.

THEODORE PARKER (1810–1860), UNITARIAN MINISTER IN BOSTON

+++

There are two paths to sainthood — holy orders and marriage.

THOMAS MERTON (1915–1968), CISTERCIAN MONK

+++

You know when this marriage thing was invented,
people didn't live as long as they do now.

A YOUNG MAN IN 2008

+++

Marriage is neither heaven nor hell; it is simply purgatory.

ABRAHAM LINCOLN (1809–1865)

How can a man who is married have any troubles?
... If he is poor, his wife helps him work.
She saves his money and wastes nothing at all.
Anything which her husband wants pleases her as well.
Not once does she say "No," when he says "Yes."
"Do this" says he; "Done" says she.
Oh, blissful state of wedlock!

"THE MERCHANT'S TALE", *THE CANTERBURY TALES*
GEOFFREY CHAUCER (1340–1400)

+++

May Jesus Christ send us husbands meek, young, and lusty abed, and the luck to outlast them. I also pray Jesus to hasten the death of those who will not be ruled by their wives.

"THE WIFE OF BATH", *THE CANTERBURY TALES*
GEOFFREY CHAUCER

Be warned! The descendants of the Merchant and the Wife of Bath are alive and well.

+++

Every marriage can be shown to include within it sufficient grounds for divorce ... every marital pair are potentially incompatible and could easily separate, if their relationship were regarded in a certain way ... Whether they have been married five years, fifteen, or fifty, the hazards and risks are inevitable, recurrent, perennial.

SONIA RUDIKOFF
COMMENTARY, JUNE 1973, P. 61

**It is not your love that sustains your marriage,
but your marriage that sustains your love.**

DIETRICH BONHOEFFER (1906–1945)
FROM A LETTER SMUGGLED OUT OF
THE PRISON WHERE HE WAS HELD

+++

**Arranged marriages endure much better than
Western marriages because individual happiness
is not the only thing in the world.
In an arranged marriage the idea of happiness is bound up
with family obligation and the social contract.**

A PROFESSOR OF COMPARATIVE RELIGIONS

+++

Love means never having to say you're sorry.

ERICH SEGAL (1937–2016)
WRITER, RUNNER, TEACHER, FATHER

+++

Erich Segal was wrong. Why? Because in the course of any marriage the two will fail each other many times. Each failure causes at least some pain and resentment. At that point the two stand at a crossroads, that is, a choice between a fight or forgiveness.

A good marriage is the union of two forgivenesses.

RUTH BELL GRAHAM, WIFE OF EVANGELIST BILLY GRAHAM

Forgiveness is the act of surrendering one's justified or unjustified resentment. Without such a surrender, one or both partners will in time accumulate a burden of resentment so heavy that it will crush their marriage.

How does one forgive? First by facing the consequences of not forgiving. Then by thoughtful reflection, prayer, meditation, mediation, and, at the right time, quiet conversation with the other. Sometimes the marriage endures through the immense patience of one party who knows the marriage is worth that effort.

+++

Jesus told us to love our neighbor as we love ourselves. Our spouse or partner is our first neighbor.

AN OLD PASTOR

+++

Chains do not hold a marriage together. It is threads, hundreds of tiny threads, which sew people together over the years.

SIMONE SIGNORET (1921–1985)
FRENCH MOVIE ACTRESS

+++

A marriage consists of three parties: You and I and us. You and I must take care of us.

MY FRIEND JASON

Husband and wife become each other's monastery. Their life together is a sacrament, holy to the church because of what it teaches about faithfulness and steadfastness and compassion and holy hilarity and tenderness and hospitality and the sanctity of everyday things. Their marriage is a continual conversion to their life together.

HUGH FEISS OSB,
MONASTERY OF THE ASCENSION,
ESSENTIAL MONASTIC WISDOM, HARPER, 1999

+++

Your marriage is a living, breathing koan.

This is what their counselor told Kate and Drew, as reported by Kate Braestrup in her excellent book, *Marriage and Other Acts of Charity*, an account of marriage as it is really lived.

+++

My wife said to me the other day, after a knock-down, drag-out fight over interior decoration, "I don't love you any more." And I said to her, "So what else is new?" She really didn't love me then, which was perfectly normal. She will love me some other time — I think, I hope. It's possible.

If she had wanted to terminate the marriage, to carry it past the point of no return, she would have had to say "I don't respect you any more." Now that would be terminal.

One of the many unnecessary American catastrophes going on right now ... is all the people who are getting divorced because they don't love each other anymore. That is like trading in a car when the ashtrays are full. When you don't respect your mate anymore, that's when the transmission is shot and there's a crack in the engine block."

KURT VONNEGUT (1922–2007)
FATES WORSE THAN DEATH, 1991, BERKELEY PUBLISHING GROUP

+++

A perfect marriage is two imperfect people who won't give up on each other.

NOTE ON A REFRIGERATOR DOOR

+++

Minnie Mae and I have had several marriages during our life together.

DON MURRAY (1924–2006), "OVER SIXTY," *THE BOSTON GLOBE*

Don Murray said a lot in that sentence. Every marriage is a series of marriages. The first marriage may be an experiment in living together, while the couple test their compatibility. At some point they split or stick. A decision to raise children usually leads to a wedding.

The next marriage may come with the arrival of children who consume vast amounts of energy, attention, money, patience, and grey matter. This leaves parents less time for each other when they really need more. One great remedy for this is a weekly night out for supper and conversation. Some do this by trading nights with other couples, paying a baby sitter or inviting grandparents for extended visits.

Children may not arrive, but new marriages will. Promotions, bankruptcy, medical crises, aging parents or moves to a new city or country will change the marital landscape. So will fatigue, boredom, inattention, or interference from other parties.

When children leave home, parents may rediscover each other. This can lead to the best years of their marriage.

Each transition from one marriage to another is a time of testing. A capable counselor, a supportive extended family, and institutions like a good church, AA, or therapy groups can help a couple meet these challenges.

Usually there comes the time when one partner begins to fail and the other becomes the caretaker. This is followed by the last stage when the failing partner dies, and the survivor lives alone, for this too is part of marriage.

Bruce,
I'm getting married
this year,
and I hope it's you.

Should I Marry and Whom?

I was looking for someone exactly like her but totally different.

A YOUNG MAN REPORTED IN *THE BOSTON GLOBE*, 4 OCT. 2014

+++

He sat down beside me, and I felt like I was at home.
He's so normal and nice.
We spend hours talking about nothing.

A YOUNG WOMAN TALKING TO AN OLDER WOMAN
AS THEY CROSSED THE BOSTON PUBLIC GARDEN

+++

Mother:
Why is he answering your phone? I thought you left him.

Daughter:
Oh, Ma, we tried breaking up but it just didn't work out.

Mother: When are you going to fall in love?
Son: I don't know, Mom. I just seem to fall in lust.

+++

"... a girl and a soldier, who by their way of walking, seemed to have no destination but each other ..."

"MYSTERIOUS KOR" BY ELIZABETH BOWEN
LONDON STORIES, ED. JERRY WHITE, P. 318

+++

Words of warning are appropriate.

Better well hung than ill wed.

OLIVIA IN *TWELFTH NIGHT*
WILLIAM SHAKESPEARE

+++

"V" is now the scarlet letter

A YOUNG WOMAN AFTER TWO OFFENSIVE ONLINE DATES

To the ladies: Any young Lady between the ages of Eighteen and Twenty-five of a Middling Stature, brown Hair, regular features, and with a Lively Brisk Eye, of Good Morals … possessed of 3 or 400 pounds entirely at her own Disposal and where there will be no necessity of going through the tiresome Talk of addressing Parents or Guardians … (may) by leaving a Line directed for A.W. at the British Coffee House in King Street appointing where an interview may be had will meet with a Person who flatters himself that he shall not be thought disagreeable.

ADVERTISEMENT IN *THE BOSTON EVENING POST*, FEB. 23, 1759

The author of the above ad might be a descendant of Chaucer's merchant.

+++

Grandmother:
Why haven't you married that guy?

Granddaughter:
I don't know how to bring up marriage in our conversations.

Grandmother:
What? You've been exchanging bodily fluids with this guy for a year and you can't talk about marriage? What happened to your wiles of womanhood?

The matter of dispositions should be tested in every possible way [before marriage] without the risk of incurring irreparable wounds. It is much better in love affairs to be slightly wounded before battle than to be mortally wounded in the conflict of domestic infelicities.

JOSEPH E. PARSIFAL
TWELVE CONSIDERATIONS FOR MARRIAGE, 1930

+++

When you are of any age to think of settling, let your affections be placed on a steady, sober, religious man who will be tender and careful of you at all times. Do not marry a very young man, as you know not how he may turn out.

ELIZABETH KENNEDY, WRITING TO HER DAUGHTERS IN 1801

+++

Encouragement is also appropriate

She: But if we get married, what if my cancer comes back?

He: What does that have to do with anything?

They sooner met, but they look'd;
No sooner look'd but they lov'd;
No sooner lov'd, but they sigh'd;
No sooner sigh'd, but they asked one another the reason;
No sooner knew the reason, but they sought the remedy;
And in these degrees they have made
a pair of stairs to marriage...

AS YOU LIKE IT, ACT V, SCENE 2,
WILLIAM SHAKESPEARE (1564–1616)

+++

Bruce, I'm getting married this year, and I hope it's you.

LELIA, AFTER THEY HAD LIVED TOGETHER FOR 16 YEARS

+++

Syed and Sayeeda both felt that marriage was too large a step to risk going on their own limited experience. So they left the selection to a great uncle, the primary matchmaker for her family who had arranged her parents' marriage. In their families they had learned to trust the experience of the matchmaker more than their own.

Sometimes a good fight can clear the air, if it's a good fight. For example, a middle-aged couple walking on a street in Boston began this conversation:

He: This would be a good time to move to Florida.

She: Yes, and it would be a good time to get married too.

He: Do you really think so?

She: Yes, I really think so.

An argument followed and she moved to the other side of the street.

She: You'd better think about the next thing you say to me because if it doesn't have marriage in it, you won't be seeing me anymore.

He: Well, are we going to be shouting at each other?

She: I hope not.

He crossed the street to her side, they got married and moved to Florida where they enjoyed happy and passionate years together.

\+ + +

And sometimes there's a surprising discovery.

Charles, an old man, and Ellen, a young woman, were chatting at a family reunion about her long relationship with a cousin in the family. Charles asked Ellen, "How long have you two been living together?" Ellen said, "Ten years." Charles asked, "How come you haven't gotten married?" Here is how Ellen later reported her response to Charles:

"This wedding is all Charles' fault. When he asked me why we weren't married, I went into a whole diatribe about how marriage is just a social contract. I said that Bob and I have a commitment, and I feel that if we got married, it would be less of a commitment because right now I can leave at any time. Yet I really do want to be with this man, but I'm not connected to him by a piece of paper. I can leave at any time but I want to be with him because I love him so much. This marriage thing is so societal. Charles said, 'You don't know what you don't know.' I was rendered ..."

She was going to say "speechless," but her voice was drowned out by the laughter of the wedding guests at the rehearsal dinner. Perhaps Charles' comment suggested to Ellen a depth of relationship which marriage might make possible.

You don't
marry someone
just because
you love them,
but because
you respect them.

What Should I Know Before I Decide?

The time of courting is a good time for the engaged couple to hear what the married say about marriage.

Get married with both eyes open. Then close one eye.

A GREEK PRIEST

+++

Choose your love. Then love your choice.

WHO TOLD ME THIS? I DON'T REMEMBER.

+++

Anyone who can't deal with loneliness shouldn't get married.

A CHARACTER IN *WETHERBY*,
A BRITISH FILM 1985

+++

The first love is drunken. When the intoxication wears off, the real married love begins.

MARTIN LUTHER (1483–1546)

You don't marry someone just because you love them, but because you respect them.

OUR DENTIST'S AUNT

+++

What would I tell an engaged couple?
It's not going to be what you think.

A WIDOW AFTER FIFTY YEARS OF MARRIAGE

+++

A couple in love cannot know how much more they will learn about each other, for they are marrying not only each other but each other's families, histories, and values. They are also marrying each other's unconscious, which they themselves do not know. Sooner or later those unconscious selves will emerge and must be dealt with.

When marrying, ask each other if you will be able to converse with each other into old age. Everything else is ephemeral.

FREDERICK NIETSCHE (1844–1900)

+++

Marriage is like the stock market. You shouldn't get into it, if you can't afford to lose a little.

A BRIDE OF FIVE YEARS

It's important to find out what makes the other laugh, and then help to make that happen. Laughing aligns two minds and helps them move beyond their stuck places. It lets people be more present to each other, to play and enjoy each other.

MY FRIEND, MEGAN

+++

Laughter is important because nothing improves lovemaking like a sense of humor.

AGAIN, I DON'T RECALL WHO SAID THIS

+++

Couples need the most help during the first year of their marriage.

KAREN KAYSER, AUTHOR OF
WHEN LOVE DIES, 1993

+++

The difference between marital and martial is a misplaced "I."

AN OLD ADAGE

+++

We're going to have some fights and you're going to win half of them.

ROGER TO MARGARET BEFORE THEIR MARRIAGE

The age of eighteen is the best time for women to marry, and the age of thirty-seven or less for men.

ARISTOTLE (364–322 BCE)

+++

By all means marry. If you marry a good wife, you'll be happy. If you don't, you'll become a philosopher.

SOCRATES (D. 399 BCE)

Socrates' wife Xantippe gets a bad rap in most reports, but we've never heard her side of the story

+++

Good marriages are made between those who, if they must, can live without each other.

AN OLD HUSBAND

+++

As God's chosen ones, holy and beloved, clothe yourselves with compassion, kindness, humility, meekness, and patience. Bear with one another, and if one has a complaint against the other, forgive each other as the Lord has forgiven you.

ST. PAUL'S LETTER TO THE CHRISTIANS IN COLOSSIANS (3:12)

St. Paul wrote those words to people who were creating a new religious community. It's good advice for a couple, who are themselves creating a new community.

First look at the house;
Then look at the bed;
Then look at the money;
Then look at the man.

ADVICE TO A PROSPECTIVE BRIDE IN ANCIENT CHINA

+++

Let there be spaces in your togetherness.

KAHLIL GIBRAN (1883–1931)
LEBANESE POET, ARTIST, ÉMIGRÉ

+++

The Lover desires the perfection of the Beloved,
which requires, among other things,
the liberation of the Beloved from the Lover.

RAINER MARIE RILKE (1875–1926)

+++

You wives, strong as camels, stand up for your rights.
Don't allow men to do injustices to you.
And, weak wives, feeble in battle, be fierce as tigers.

CHAUCER'S POSTSCRIPT TO "THE CLERK'S TALE,"
THE CANTERBURY TALES, CA. 1400

With this ring
I thee wed …
so long as
we both shall live.

The Wedding

**Where you go, I will go. Where you lodge, I will lodge.
Your people shall be my people, and your god my god.**

RUTH 1:16

Ruth made this promise to her mother-in-law, Naomi. She kept this promise not just to Naomi but also to Boaz, whom she later married.

+++

**Set me as a seal upon your heart, as a seal upon your arm,
for love is as strong as death, passion as fierce as the grave.**

THE SONG OF SONGS 8:6–7

+++

**You must come to my wedding.
I have made the angels laugh and the devils weep.**

MARTIN LUTHER (1483–1546)

+++

When the unlucky host ran out of wine at the wedding party, Jesus turned a hundred gallons of water into wine that proved even better than what the guests first consumed. (John 2:1–11) It seems that Jesus wanted everyone there to be happy. It may also explain why Jesus so often described the kingdom of God as a feast.

"You can have a small wedding, you can have a short wedding, and you can have an inexpensive wedding, but you cannot have a simple wedding." I've said this to several couples, because a wedding is the door to a state of being which is anything but simple.

Marriage is a union of differences as well as similarities. Guests at a wedding rarely discuss these differences, but everyone knows they are there. Their silence on this subject may explain the unspoken nervousness at even the happiest of weddings.

We sensibly felt the Lord with us and joining us, the sense whereof remained with us all our lifetime, and was of very good service and very comfortable to us on all occasions.

THOMAS AND MARY ELLWOOD
QUAKERS MARRIED IN 1669

+++

Long ago at the beginning of our history as a people, our Torah records that God said to Abram and Sara "… Be thou a blessing that all the world may be blessed through you."

RABBI RONALD WEISS OF WELLESLEY, MA
TO A YOUNG COUPLE AT THEIR WEDDING

+++

Now we're no longer "the boys." Now we're like everyone else.

JON AFTER HIS MARRIAGE TO MARTIN

I can't often feel the love and promises I made at our wedding, making them before people who loved and trusted me. I had no idea what I was promising, how I would fulfill those promises, or what I would be facing in the years ahead. But promising them anyway.

MY SISTER, JUDY

+++

With gratitude for our years together, I vow to stand by you, through whatever happiness or difficulty may come our way, until death separates us. I pray that the consolation of our mutual love will allow us to grow in wisdom and compassion, not only to each other, but to all the world around us.

DAVE O'NEAL AND ERIC BRUS
SAID THESE VOWS IN 2013

Four years later Dave suffered a major stroke. Since that stroke, Dave and Eric have attempted day by day to honor their marriage vows. Each in his own way is a stroke survivor, and each is a caregiver for the other.

+++

So for me this covenant with you, this publically witnessed tradition, came to feel important in my imagining us together, as a gesture that honors our life, honors our good fortune in having found each other, the leap of faith that long-term love requires.

MIMI TO DON AT THEIR WEDDING

David and Janice invited their grown sons and extended families to their farm in Maine for Thanksgiving Day. After dinner David dinged on his glass to get everyone's attention. The following conversation ensued.

David: I have a question to ask Janice.
Janice, will you marry me?
Janice: Do I have to change my name?
David: No.
Janice: When?
David: Right now.
Janice: OK.

Immediately, their eldest son, recently licensed to conduct one marriage that year, stood and pronounced them husband and wife. At this time David and Janice had lived together for forty-five years.

+++

Our minister said the wedding vows and we repeated them after her. When she said, "To love and to cherish until we are parted by death," I looked into the face of my older husband-to-be and said to myself: "It does not matter if you die within a week. You will be my only love."

They were still married many years later when the bride told me this.

+++

At the rehearsal dinner the tearful bride drew her husband away from the festivities and asked, "Do I have to get married tomorrow?" "No, of course not," he answered. She continued, "But if we do get married, can I get divorced later?" "Yes, of course," he said. She told me of this conversation fifty-four years later, her husband listening with a slight smile on his face.

Blessed art Thou, O Lord our God, Ruler of the universe, who has created bride and groom, joy and gladness, daylight and cheer, love and harmony, peace and companionship. Blessed art Thou, O Lord, who has made the groom and the bride rejoice in each other,

FROM THE JEWISH WEDDING SERVICE

+++

I didn't marry you because you were perfect. I didn't even marry you because I loved you. I married you because you gave me a promise. ... That promise made up for your faults. And the promise I gave you made up for mine. Two imperfect people got married, and it was the promise that made the marriage.

THE SKIN OF OUR TEETH BY THORNTON WILDER

+++

The traditional vows end "And thereto I pledge thee my troth." The last word is "troth," not "love." Troth means faithfulness. Faithfulness creates trust and trust makes love possible.

I first thought love
an easy thing.
Then came
the hard awakening.

Who Are We Now That We're Married?

I thought I was a basically good-natured person until I got married.

A NEW HUSBAND

+++

We had lived together for three years and thought we knew each other.

A WIFE

+++

There's a lot to get used to in the first year of marriage. One wakes up and finds a pair of pigtails on the pillow beside you that were not there before.

MARTIN LUTHER, WHO MARRIED WHEN HE WAS FORTY-TWO

The longer I live with him, the clearer it becomes that I cannot expect to understand him. Coming to this realization makes me look at him as a new person, not as the one whom I expected him to be.

A WIFE OF ALMOST FIVE DECADES.

+++

When we try to solve the puzzle of another person by waking up next to him or her every damn day for the rest of our lives, we bend ourselves to their reality and they to ours. We learn each other's respective backstories, and then we learn how those stories work in the present, minute by minute, by trial and error. Every time two strangers decide to move in together, two houses have to be rewired into one. There's going to be a lot of compromises and the building's definitely not going to be up to code, but with luck you'll have light everywhere you look.

TY BURR, COLUMNIST FOR *THE BOSTON GLOBE*

+++

I first thought love an easy thing.
Then came the hard awakening.

HAFIZ, PERSIAN POET, D. 1389

+++

Thank you, Lord, for our conversation over that painful issue. Thank you for making it possible for us to talk slowly and sadly about it. Thank you for the peace that came to us afterward.

A PRAYER AFTER CONFLICT

In all thy humors whether grave or mellow
Thou'rt such a hasty, testy, pleasant fellow;
Thou hast so much of wit and spleen about thee,
That there's no living with thee — or without thee.

FROM A LETTER WRITTEN ON AUGUST 1, 1788,
BY JUDITH SINGER SARGENT IN GLOUCESTER, MA
TO HER HUSBAND, JOHN MURRAY, IN LONDON

+++

Please sit down. Don't say anything. Don't do anything.
Just listen, listen, listen. And then give me a hug.

WHAT ONE WIFE SAYS TO HER HUSBAND WHEN SHE NEEDS TO TALK

+++

Maybe I was wrong. Maybe you talked it out of all proportion. So what? We love each other. We're together. That's what counts.

THE MESSAGE ON HER ANSWERING MACHINE
WHEN SHE WOULDN'T SPEAK TO HIM

+++

I suppose that joining a church is like marriage in that when you get into it, you find that it is the beginning, not the end, of making love work.

LETTER TO A RELIGIOUS INQUIRER 9 AUG. 1955
FLANNERY O'CONNOR (1925–1964)

He: Jean, you're a late bloomer.

She: John, you're a late appreciator.

+++

It is precisely because our love makes room for us to be who we are, rather than cutting us to fit convention, that I want to spend my life with him, as I'll affirm when we stand before the rabbi and say, I do.

The writer of these lines, a lesbian, met a man at a bar, who had hunted lions in Africa, climbed high mountains, serviced racing cars in Monaco and worked for NASA. They fell in love and were married. She still considers herself a lesbian, but is faithful to him as he is to her. Couples like these two people who know, love, and respect each other as they are redefine all definitions.

+++

Anger and disagreement are not harmful to marriage, but anger blended with contempt and defensiveness is very destructive.

DR. JOHN GOTTMAN
OF THE UNIVERSITY OF WASHINGTON

+++

It is our time apart that keeps us together.

JOHN ON HIS LIFE WITH HIS HUSBAND, BOB

John and Bob have learned that conflicts sometimes come from too much closeness. Spouses then begin to project their own angers, frustrations, sadness, and confusion onto each other. At this point they need distance. They need to cool down. They need to relearn their own identity with all its gifts and liabilities. Then they may be ready to understand and forgive each other.

+++

Because you have given her to me, O Lord, help me to see and love her as she is, not as I fear she is and not as I wish she were, but as you made her and gave her to me.

A PRAYER I SAID FOR MYSELF

+++

Real love as compared to fantasy is a harsh and dreadful thing.

FYODOR DOSTOYEVSKY (1821–1881)

The radical Catholic activist, Dorothy Day, used this quote to emphasize that true love is not a good feeling, but an act of sacrificial self-giving. St. Paul tells us that love demands patience, kindness, self-denial, trust, hope, and endurance. Such love is not for the faint of heart.

Love loves to please.

Making Love

... and they shall be one flesh, and they were both naked and were not ashamed.

GENESIS 2: 24C AND 25

+++

It is far better to be married than to be to be tortured by unsatisfied desire.

ST. PAUL WRITING TO THE CHRISTIANS IN CORINTH (CA. 50 CE)

+++

I have taken off my dress; how can I put it on again?
I have washed my feet; how can I dirty them?
My darling thrust his hand from the opening,
And my guts churned for him.

SONG OF SONGS 5: 2- 4, TRANSLATED BY
ELLEN DAVIS, PROFESSOR OF OLD TESTAMENT,
DUKE UNIVERSITY DIVINITY SCHOOL

If you can get along well out of bed, half the problems of the bed are solved.

PETER USTINOV (1921–2004)
BRITISH ACTOR, WRITER, BROADCASTER

+++

No renunciation is commanded. One eats in holiness and the table becomes an altar. ... One walks in holiness and the soft song of the herbs enters into the song of our soul. ... One dances the roundelay in holiness and a brightness illumines the gathering. A husband and wife are united in holiness, and the presence of God rests over them.

MARTIN BUBER (1878–1965)
HASIDIM, PHILOSOPHICAL LIBRARY

+++

The husband should give to his wife her conjugal rights and likewise the wife her conjugal rights to the husband. For the wife does not have authority over her own body but the husband. Likewise the husband does not have authority over his own body but the wife does.

I CORINTHIANS: 7: 3 – 5A, ST. PAUL

In a culture where husbands literally owned their wives and might enjoy extra-marital liasons with impunity, what St. Paul wrote was radical. He himself was unmarried.

My dear, I cannot tell
How it should come about
That we who loved so well,
Should turn to falling out.
But since the spring is come
With running sap and leaves,
Strong-shooting from the boughs,
And swallows in the eaves,
Since spring is come with rain
And green and hidden ditches,
We'll mend the purse of love
With quick and purposed stitches.

"THE GOOD WIFE RELENTS"
BY GWEN CLEAR

+++

Love loves to please.

FIRE OF MERCY, HEART OF THE WORD, VOL. III, P. 523
BY ERASMO LEIVA-MERIKAKIS

+++

Most like an arch – two weaknesses that lean
into each other. Two fallings become firm.

FROM "MOST LIKE AN ARCH THIS MARRIAGE"
BY JOHN CIARDI (1916–1986)

Only too much love is enough.

JOHN UPDIKE (1932–2009)

+++

The only measure of love is to love without measure.

ST. BERNARD OF CLAIRVAUX (1090–1153)
FOUNDER OF THE CISTERCIAN ORDER

+++

The only way to love anything [or anyone]
Is to realize they might be lost.

G.K. CHESTERTON (1874–1936)

+++

Strange, that at dawn
A smile remains ...
Our love untouched.

FROM THE END OF A POEM BY
MYRA SCOTT SCOVEL (1905–1994)

+++

We think of getting divorced so we can become lovers again.

A MIDDLE-AGED COUPLE

We knew nothing about sex when we got married. We each felt cheated in our first marriages, and we weren't going to miss out on this one. So we went to the library and took out books on sex, and practiced. It was great!

THE WIFE IN A SECOND MARRIAGE

+++

Carl, don't let them ever tell you that lightning doesn't strike twice in the same place.

A WIDOW WHO HAD JUST MET THE MAN SHE LATER MARRIED.

+++

The Americans who are having the most sex – and enjoying it most too – are monogamous married couples, not the unattached under thirty."

REPORT ON "SEX IN AMERICA" BASED ON INTERVIEWS WITH MORE THAN THREE THOUSAND COUPLES

+++

A couple were hiking in the White Mountains, when he said to her: "You know, dear, this is like sex. It's so much fun I don't know why we don't do it more often."

+++

You make love the best way you can.

THE BUTCHER SAID THIS TO A WOMAN BUYING A STEAK FOR HER NINETY-SIX YEAR OLD HUSBAND

We have them
all our lives.

Children

Your loving wife has had a child.

POSSIBLY THE OLDEST LETTER IN HISTORY,
WRITTEN IN CUNEIFORM ON A CLAY TABLET

+++

Children! They're either a pain in the neck or a lump in the throat.

A FRIEND'S MOTHER-IN-LAW

+++

When we got married in our early twenties, we were both intent on our careers and working overseas, so we had no interest in having children. But in my early thirties when I saw a woman carrying her plump, brown baby over her shoulder, something in me changed. Then and there I knew I wanted a child. Eventually my husband agreed, and we had two sons.

A FRIEND

Being a grandmother is truly a blessed role ... it has been so long since I held my daughter as a newborn that I can only compare my experience of holding her daughter to once holding a wild osprey fledgling. Once the bird felt the slow breathing of my chest against its body, it fell asleep. So my granddaughter and I had similar hours together, giving her parents a chance for that longed-for shower.

A NEW GRANDMOTHER

+++

**People think they have babies.
But we don't; we have people,
and we have them all our lives,
and we never stop worrying about them.
Never.**

DONNA LEON (1942–), *FALLING IN LOVE*, P. 58

+++

A mother is only as happy as her unhappiest child.

A MOTHER

A baby is nothing if not a reservoir of details.

MICHELLE OBAMA IN HER AUTOBIOGRAPHY
BECOMING, RANDOM HOUSE 2018

+++

When we vowed "in sickness and in health, for better or for worse," we imagined that we were talking about each other. I thought to myself, "I can do that." Of course, I would stand by him in difficult times, and that was good enough for that day. But there's no way to prepare for the pain of a child being very sick. It has since struck me how much simpler things looked then.

A MOTHER FOR MORE THAN TWENTY YEARS

+++

I didn't know what a wonderful wife I had until the kids went to college. Those rascals were holding us captive!

A FRIEND WHOM I MET AT THE GYM

+++

It was only after our children left home that we became again the main interest in each other's lives.

AN OLDER WIFE

The most important thing a husband can do for his children is to love their mother.

THEODORE HESBURGH SJ (1917–2015)
PRESIDENT OF NOTRE DAME UNIVERSITY

✦✦✦

Thank you for getting married.
Thank you for staying married.
Thank you for giving me a great home
and a family to grow up in,
and a sister and a brother.

ON THEIR 49TH ANNIVERSARY THEIR YOUNGEST DAUGHTER LEFT THIS MESSAGE ON THEIR ANSWERING MACHINE.

✦✦✦

If we'd had children, we wouldn't have had the life we have. They just never came. By now we'd be grandparents and that would be nice, but we're not unfulfilled.

JULIA CHILD (1912–2004)

Few things test a marriage more than the death of a child. I write this because all parents live under the shadow of their children's possible death, an event that drives some parents apart and brings others together. A couple who lost their adolescent son more than ten years ago told me the following:

What often makes the difference is the parents' ability to love one another as they grieve, to trust that each of them feels the loss deeply, though they may not display it in the same ways, and to find support in family, friends, and community. There are few events in life that test faith as much as losing a child, but faith, trust, and the couple's love for each other can help with the loss. Life will never be the same after losing a child, but it does not mean that a couple will lose their marriage as well.

I learned this myself one day when I hailed a cab and met a mystic. Wearing silver-framed glasses and sporting a shaggy grey beard, he drove like someone trying to catch up with a vision just ahead of him. At the end of the ride he turned and looked me in the eye and said,"There is only one miracle in this world. A father and mother lose their child, and they do not curse God."

What did I know
of love's austere
and homely offices?

The Work of Marriage

I know that people look at me and Barak as the ideal relationship ... But whoa, people, slow down. Marriage is hard work.

MICHELLE OBAMA IN AN INTERVIEW WITH OPRAH WINFREY
REPORTED IN THE *OPRAH MAGAZINE*, DECEMBER, 2018, P.173

+++

My lord Katie plants our fields and pastures and sells cows.

MARTIN LUTHER (1483–1546)

She also managed an orchard producing apples, pears, grapes, nuts, and peaches. She fished trout, carp, pike, and perch from the local pond. She fed frequent invasions of her husband's students and colleagues. She directed the household staff, gave birth to six children, and raised them too.

+++

We have learned to navigate the distances between her temperament and mine, but we know the right place is somewhere in the middle. Grace has helped us more than once and so do prayers.

MY FRIEND AND COLLEAGUE, DAVID

Earlier in this book you read "marriage is a three-ring circus." Here's the rest of that quote: "the engagement ring, the wedding ring, and suffering."

Suffering? You bet! In marriage we live with each other's fears, anxieties, nightmares, sins, and sickness. We may try to change each other, but eventually we learn that our husband, wife, or partner, like us, changes slowly or not at all. We must live with each other as graciously as we can, and sometimes, to our regret, ungraciously.

The Christian church calls this work "bearing one's cross." It is work, but it is not masochism. As we learn to do this work, we become stronger and realize that this may be the most important way we can love our beloved.

Robert Hayden wrote a poem about his father who rose every morning in the dark, split kindling, and made a fire to warm the house. He daily shined the shoes of his indifferent adolescent son. At the end of his poem Robert Hayden asks, "What did I know of love's austere and homely offices?"

Sweeping the floor, making supper, scrubbing table tops, washing dishes, paying bills, balancing the check book, taking phone calls, putting new batteries in the thermostat, calling the service man, and listening, listening, listening — all these are "love's austere and homely offices."

The hardest act of love is to give up part of oneself. When he was thirteen, Martin promised his medically-phobic father that he would never see a doctor or go to a hospital. When he met Jon, twenty years his junior, they fell in love and lived together for thirty-three years. During all that time Martin kept his promise to his father. When Martin fell grievously ill, Jon pleaded with him to get medical help. Martin finally consented, but died a week later in the hospital. Jon remembers Martin's consent to be hospitalized as his final act of love.

Love is
the exchange
of gifts.

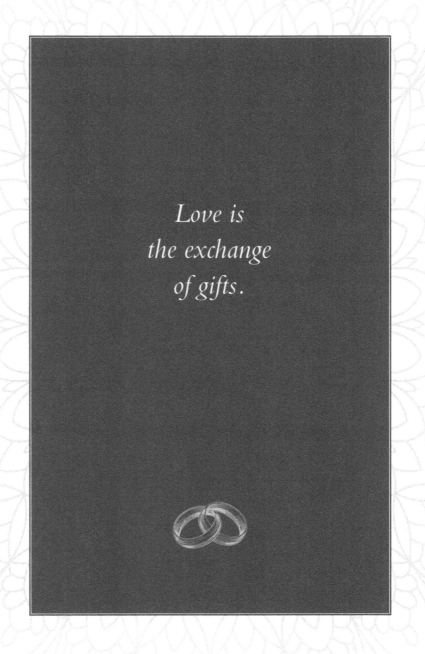

For Better

There is nothing more noble or admirable
than when two people see eye to eye,
keep house as man and wife,
confounding their enemies
and delighting their friends.

HOMER (CA.850 BC)

+++

I think that when friends marry, they are safe.

THE LAST LINE OF *O PIONEERS*, BY WILLA CATHER (1873–1947)

+++

Home is the place where you have to get to
when you're cold, sick, or discouraged.
I imagine a good husband is "home" for his wife.

YE GODS AND LITTLE FISHES, P. 341
BY OUR FRIEND, MARY ANNE MOORE

+++

I felt married before we got married and
more free to be myself after we got married.

MY FRIEND LYNN

My wife says that if I ever decide to leave,
she's coming with me.

JON BON JOVI (1962–), SINGER, COMPOSER, PHILANTHROPIST

+++

If ever there were one, then surely we.
If ever man were loved by wife, then ye;
If ever wife was happy in a man,
Compare with me, ye women, if ye can.

ANNE BRADSTREET (1612–1672)

+++

Sleep … is still most perfect when it is shared with the beloved. The warmth, the security and peace of soul, the utter comfort from the touch of the other, knits the sleep, so that it takes the body and soul completely in its healing.

D.H. LAWRENCE (1885–1930)

+++

Love is the exchange of gifts.

ST. IGNATIUS OF LOYOLA (1491–1556)

+++

I used to think that there were lots of people I could be married to. But the more things I share with my wife, the harder it is for me to imagine being married to anyone else.

THE HUSBAND IN AN ARRANGED MARRIAGE

When you look back upon this day, I hope you will agree that on this day you loved each other least, because by then your love will have grown so much.

SO SAID THE PRIEST TO JACK AND SHEILA
AT THEIR WEDDING

+++

Since I love, I cannot doubt that I am loved, anymore than I can doubt that I love.

ST. BERNARD (1090–1153)
ABBOT AT THE ABBEY IN CLAIRVAUX, FRANCE

+++

He who weds a good wife, it is as if he had fulfilled all the Commandments.

THE TALMUD
(AND SHE WHO WEDS A GOOD HUSBAND)

+++

**Men and women who learn to live through the long years get to know one another's failings.
But they also come to know what is worthy of respect and admiration in those they live with and in themselves.**

THIS I REMEMBER, P. 345
BY ELEANOR ROOSEVELT (1884–1962)

She (falling asleep): Did the doctor send a bill
for looking at my boobs?

He (just as sleepy): No, honey, just a thank you note.

+++

He (on leaving the party): Congratulations
for not saying what you were going to say.

She (laughing): How did you know what I was going to say?

He: How long have we been married?

+++

You are polishing me like old wood.
At night we curl together like two rings.

"MARRIAGE AMULET"
BY NANCY WILLARD (1936–2017)

+++

You are my thirteenth chapter of First Corinthians … Without you, my dear, I would not have had love … You are the one part of me which would be lacking if I were alone … It is only in our union that we form a complete human being … And that is why, my dear, you will never lose me on this earth.

HELMUT, COUNT VON MOLTKE (1907–1945)
FROM A LETTER WRITTEN TO HIS WIFE ON THE
NIGHT BEFORE HIS EXECUTION BY THE GESTAPO

It is in fact a great consolation in this life

to have someone to whom you can be
united in the intimate embrace of love;

in whom your spirit can rest:
to whom you can pour out your soul;

in whose delightful company you can
take comfort in the midst of sadness;

in whose most friendly bosom you can
find peace in so many worldly setbacks;

to whose loving heart you can open your innermost
thoughts as freely as to your self; through whose kisses,
as by some medicine, you are cured of the sickness of worry;

who weeps with you in sorrow, rejoices with you in joy,
and wonders with you in doubt; whom you draw by the
fetters of love into that inner room of your soul;

with whom you rest, just the two of you,
in the sleep of peace far from the world's noise,

to whom you join and unite yourself
so that soul mixes with soul and two become one.

FROM "THE MIRROR OF LOVE"
BY ST. AELRED (1109–1167)
ABBOT OF THE MONASTERY AT RIVAULX

… accepting
the unacceptable …

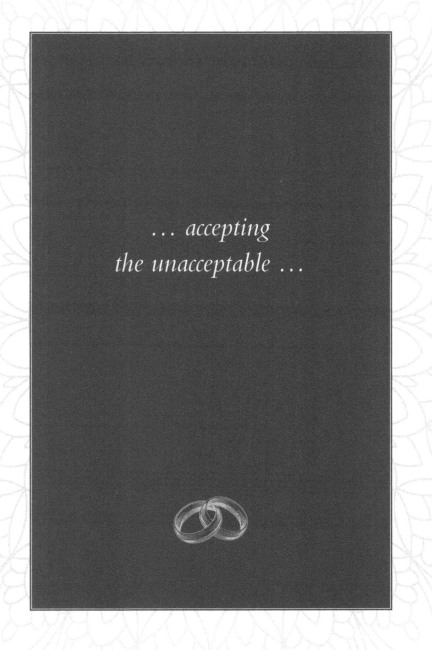

For Worse

What a lot of trouble there is in marriage! Adam made a mess of our nature. Think of all the squabbles he and Eve must have had in the course of their nine hundred years. Eve would say, "You ate the apple," and Adam would retort, "You gave it to me."

MARTIN LUTHER (1483–1546)

+++

You have no right to the joys of marriage if you have not experienced its pains.

SOMEONE, BUT I CAN'T REMEMBER WHO

+++

He doesn't have Alzheimer's. I do.

THE WIFE OF A DEMENTED HUSBAND

+++

It takes two to tango, or tangle.

MARRIAGE CAN BE A DANCE OR A DUEL.

The difference between a failed and a successful marriage is the ability to accept the unacceptable.

A SINGLE MAN TWICE MARRIED, TWICE DIVORCED

+++

The only thing that helped me survive some of our difficult times was imagining my husband in his coffin. When I thought of the things I wouldn't have to deal with anymore, I realized that I would also miss them.

A WIFE OF MANY YEARS

+++

I was a high school student, standing in our kitchen, and listening to my parents argue. I could see that they were talking past each other, not to each other, and I thought to myself, "It's all over."

A FRIEND

+++

I can't go to pieces. He needs me.

A WIFE CARING FOR HER STROKE-SMITTEN HUSBAND AFTER FIFTY-SIX YEARS OF MARRIAGE

Love anything [or anyone] and your heart will be wrung and possibly broken.

CLIVE STAPLES LEWIS (1898–1963)
PROFESSOR OF ENGLISH AT OXFORD

+++

Am I married? Am I a man? And is not a man stupid? Yes, I am married—a wife, children, house, the whole catastrophe.

ZORBA THE GREEK
NIKOS KAZANTZAKIS (1883–1957)

+++

My daughter says her fiance's one fault is leaving food in the sink drain. All I can say to that is "Wait till next year, honey, and see if your list isn't longer."

FROM "BEYOND BREAKFAST"
BY ANNE BERNAYS

A divorce is like amputation;
you survive
but there's less of you.

Divorce

Suppose a man marries a woman, but in some way she does not please him because he finds something objectionable about her. He writes her a bill of divorce, hands it to her, and sends her out of his house.

DEUTERONOMY 24:1

+++

Do not allow anyone to be faithless to the wife of his youth. For I hate divorce, says the Lord, the God of Israel.

MALACHI 2: 15B–16A

+++

Only because your minds were closed did Moses give you permission to divorce your wives, but it was not like that in the beginning. I tell you, if a man divorces his wife for any cause other than unchastity, and marries another, he is committing adultery.

JESUS IN MATTHEW 19:8–9

When I began my ministry in Sudbury MA in 1957, the Commonwealth allowed divorce if one partner confessed to adultery. Incompatible but faithful couples had to decide which of them would take the rap. Usually, and by mutual consent, it was the husband.

+++

If you think that marriage isn't forever, try divorce.

AN EX-WIFE

+++

I was walking like a zombie without any life in me. I almost died … until I started to look for something that I did not know. I just believed for some reason there must be an answer somewhere. I guess God's love was stronger than my anger. I am OK now and happy that a special strength came from above and directed me to where I am today.

A WOMAN MANY YEARS AFTER HER DIVORCE

+++

Sometimes I feel as if I had failed not just my ex and our kids, but God as well. After all we made our promises before Him.

A MAN MANY YEARS AFTER HIS DIVORCE

They [his former wives] never learned to live with the horn.

LOUIS ARMSTRONG (1901–1971)

Wives and husbands have to live with each other's jobs, obsessions, memories, fears, and callings that, like Satchmo's horn, don't go away.

Perhaps my own deepest failure in marriage was how often my ambition to succeed as a minister and my anxiety about earning money caused me to give time, attention, and concern to my church and denomination that I should have given to my wife. If I had done otherwise, I could have saved both of us a lot of suffering. To her immense credit my wife stayed the course with me.

+++

We're trying to decide whether to get divorced or have a baby.

SOMEONE I MET WHILE HIKING

I wish I'd said to her, "If that's your choice, get divorced. The baby will not keep you together."

+++

I lost my wife and gained a friend.

His new friend was his ex-wife.

After I'd lived a year by myself
I realized not everything was his fault.

A WIFE, HAPPILY SEPARATED, BUT STILL MARRIED

+++

For Sale:
One wedding dress, Size 9
Used Once By Mistake

AD IN *UNCLE HENRY*'S CLASSIFIEDS

+++

Every divorce is the
death of a small civilization.

PAT CONROY (1945–2016)

+++

Alimony is the ransom which the happy pay to the damned.

HENRY LOUIS MENCKEN (1880–1956)
JOURNALIST, CRITIC, BACHELOR, AND CRANK

+++

I don't know if I have done a brave thing
or been a damn fool.

A HUSBAND IN THE PROCESS OF DIVORCE

We drove to the court house together.

THE EX-HUSBAND

+++

I think I have trusted letting grace flow into my life
by deciding last year to end a marriage
in which two souls were being crushed.

BILL

+++

Soon we will file for divorce. It is mutual, it is amicable, and the right path for both of us, but it is sad. Accepting this is eased by the abiding love of a Higher Power that I have been permitted to invent for myself, having grown up without religion. Replacing fear with faith gives me courage to walk this path with kindness and hope for what will come.

A HUSBAND AFTER MANY YEARS OF MARRIAGE

+++

We get along better now that we're divorced. It's like riding our bicycles side by side, sometimes one leading, sometimes the other, and both going in the same direction. But you weld those two bicycles together, and you've got trouble.

THE EX-HUSBAND

My friend went to a court-ordered therapy session for divorcing husbands. After hearing the other men complaining about their wives, he called his wife and said, "Thank God, it's you I'm divorcing."

+++

**A divorce is like amputation;
you survive, but there's less of you.**

MARGARET ATWOOD

+++

I asked a friend of mine "Why did you two remarry after being divorced for eleven years?" He said, "It took us eleven years to become the people we wanted to be for each other.

+++

Here is a prayer that I wrote for a couple who were divorcing:

Dear Lord, I pray for my friends, and . I ask that you guide them in the journey into their separate lives. Teach them to part in peace and live apart in peace, and may that peace bless their children, their families, their friends, and colleagues. This we ask through him who gives us that peace which this world cannot give. Amen.

Yet charity in full strength
lives between them.

Marital Chastity

Chastity in marriage? Yes. Pregnancy, menstruation, abstinence as birth control, spiritual disciplines, professional travel, impotence, ill health, or disaffection may interrupt the natural rituals of love-making. Such challenges are occasions to learn more about one's marriage. St. Paul, though unmarried, reminds us that most couples should not prolong such periods of abstinence.

Do not deny each other except by agreement for a set time to devote yourselves to prayer and then come together again.

ST. PAUL, I CORINTHIANS 7: 5

+++

A nun and a priest fell in love. Faithful to their final vows, they continued celibate in their separate vocations, and the priest eventually moved overseas. Years later the nun met someone who was going to visit her old friend. Through this intermediary the nun sent the following message: "Tell him that next to God I love him best."

+++

More things belong to marriage than four bare legs in a bed.

PROVERBS BY JOHN HEYWOOD IN 1546

You might be surprised by the next quotation. I preface it by explaining that the word "fucking" in contemporary usage connotes aggression or crude indifference. For Lawrence it meant real and intimate affection.

So I love chastity now, because it is the peace that comes of fucking ... And when the real spring comes, when the drawing together comes, then we can fuck the little flame brilliant and yellow. But not now, not yet. Now is the time to be chaste, it is so good to be chaste, like a river of cool water in my soul. I love the chastity now that it flows between us.

FROM *LADY CHATTERLEY'S LOVER*
D.H. LAWRENCE (1885–1930)

+++

But now in an old marriage, though the glow of full age has withered between husband and wife, yet charity in full strength lives between them.

"ON THE GOOD OF MARRIAGE"
ST. AUGUSTINE (354–430)

+++

A devout couple after much discussion decided to enter separate religious orders but did not dissolve their marriage. They lived this way until the wife fell fatally ill. At the husband's request his wife's abbess gave him permission to live in their convent and care for his wife. This he did until she died, and he then returned to his own order.

Although her hair
was white,
he still saw his wife
as a young woman.

The Later Years

There's only so much you can say after fifty-five years, but we're confortable with our times of silence.

A HUSBAND

+++

Water in the stream wears down the stone,
Wind uproots the largest trees,
The continents drift,
Stars rush away from each other.
I am wearing down with each spring,
Still my love for you increases.

W. EDWARD HARRIS (1935–2012)
UNITARIAN UNIVERSALIST MINISTER

+++

He: It pains me to think of what a jerk I was when we got married.

She: Maybe that's what getting married is — deciding what kind of a jerk you want to work things out with. When you work things out together, it gives you something.

She: I don't think he should make himself
a martyr taking care of her.

Her cousin: She stood beside him when he was working. Now
she's failing, and it's his turn. If he's a martyr, it's for love.

+++

Almighty God who has promised us that most excellent gift
of charity, we bless and praise thee for the years of love and
loyalty, which thy servants _____ and _____ have
known together, and we pray that they may continue
in thy peace and grow in thy grace.

FROM THE KING'S CHAPEL PRAYER BOOK

+++

"When John and I were considering how to celebrate our
fortieth anniversary, we decided to rent a villa in southern
France. We invited cherished friends from the past and
present, and had a wonderful time together.

At the celebration party, one guest said to me,
'You two have had forty happy years together.' I said,
'Well, more accurately, We've been happily married
for thirty years.' The guest looked puzzled.

'Three fourths of our forty years have been very good,'
I continued. 'The other fourth? Well, not to be worried about!'
'Seventy-five percent is damn good,' said my friend,
'Let's drink to that!' And we did."

REV. GWEN LANGUEDOC BUEHRENS

While a friend of mine was staffing the registration desk at a conference, an elderly man came up to her and said, "My wife is supposed to meet me here, but I need to go outside for a few minutes. Tell her I'll be right back." My friend asked, "How will I know her?" The man said, "She's tall, wearing a light green suit, and she has red hair." Soon after he left a tall woman wearing a light green suit came to the desk and asked for her husband. Although her hair was white, my friend delivered her husband's message. She could see that he still saw his wife as a young woman.

After months of silence,
he spoke his last words
to his wife, "Thank you."

The Long Leave-Taking

Love, I'll tell you what love is. It's you at seventy-five and she at seventy-one, and each of you listening for the step in the other room, each afraid that a sudden silence, a sudden cry, could mean the end of a lifetime of talking it over.

BRIAN MOORE (1921–1999)

+++

I figured it was her or me.

AN OLD NEW ENGLAND FARMER WHO CARED FOR HIS WIFE AT HOME UNTIL HE PUT HER IN A NURSING HOME.

He may sound like a hard man, but he knew that the first job of the caretaker is to take care of the caretaker.

+++

I am not going to leave my wife a widow.

A HUSBAND WITH SERIOUS CANCER

+++

We had a very good day — behind as usual, but a kiss before dinner.

A BUSY WORKING WIFE WITH AN AGED HUSBAND

Carl: How long was it from your wife's diagnosis to her death?

My friend: Two and a half years.

Carl: How did you deal with that?

My friend: Well, it was tough. But those were the best years of our lives. We knew how precious each day was. We changed more than we ever had before.

After months of silence from Alzheimer's, he spoke his last words to his wife as she held his hand, "Thank you."

⁂

Jon: Are you feeling your mortality?

Martin: Yes, but I'm not afraid of dying. I just don't want to miss out on being with you.

⁂

Give my kindest love to my dear wife, and tell her that the uncommon union which has so long subsisted between us has been of such a nature as I trust is spiritual, and therefore will continue forever.

THE LAST REPORTED WORDS OF JONATHAN EDWARDS (1703–1758)

Before she slipped into her final sleep,
I leaned over that once strong body
and said, "I have always loved you, Janene."
To which she whispered,
"I have always loved you, Tom."
You don't have to be a grammarian to
recognize the tense of our final moment.
It was present perfect.

FROM HIS WORDS AT HER MEMORIAL SERVICE

+++

My college roommate and good friend, Bob, sometimes quizzed me about my own beliefs, but showed neither animosity toward religion nor any inclination in that direction. When I last saw him a few months before he died, he was the same old Bob. After his death his widow called me and told me that she had baptized him before he died. I asked her if this might not have been against his will. "No," she said, "He asked for it. And when I asked him why he wanted to be baptized, he said, 'Because I want to be where you and Kathy [her daughter] will be when you die."

Why did he ask for baptism? I have no explanation but I believe that his love for them was stronger than death.

Love is the
ambassador of loss.

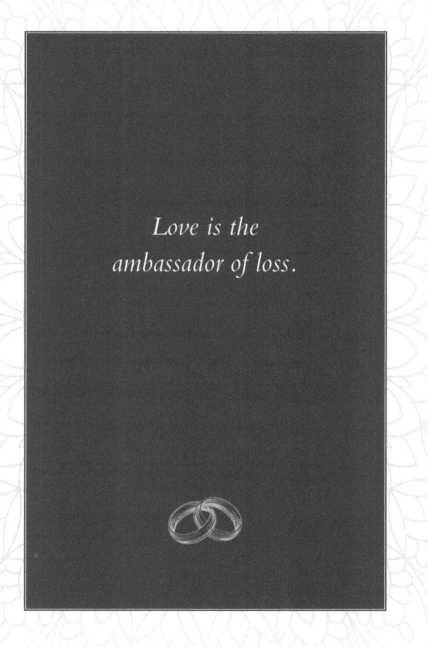

Til Death Do Us Part

His death was the death of "us,"
And when he died, "we" died.

JOYCE TYNDALL IN *THE TORONTO GLOBE AND MAIL*, 19 NOVEMBER 2014, P.10

+++

I am a death's head. Whenever I meet a happily married pair
I can feel them both thinking, "One or the other of us
must some day be as he is now."

A GRIEF OBSERVED, 1961, CLIVE STAPLES LEWIS

+++

Why am I not grieving more?
Perhaps because I was dying with her while she was dying.

A WIDOWER WHO CARED FOR HIS WIFE

+++

When my friend Horace Allen greeted the widow of an old friend just before the funeral, he said, "My dear, I'm so sorry." "It's alright, Horace," she replied. "This is the way a good marriage ends."

Love is the ambassador of loss.

JIM HAYCOX, ONCE MY SHRINK, LATER MY DEAR FRIEND

+++

Music I heard with you was more than music,
And bread I broke with you was more than bread.

CONRAD AIKEN (1889–1973)

+++

His love for me while he lived and my love for him
now must be part of Love itself.
I guess that's why our love continues.

JON

Jon's words echo the verse from the Song of Songs, "Love is as strong as death."

+++

If I'm going to be a widow, I'm going to be a merry widow.

MARLEY WATTON AFTER THE DEATH OF HER HUSBAND VAN

She could say that because she and Van had such a fine marriage

+++

Now I start my new life.

JULIA WARD HOWE (1819–1910), AFTER THE DEATH OF HER HUSBAND

I have been bereaved of the best companion of my life, who, if any severe hardship had occurred, would have been my willing partner, not just in exile and poverty, but even in death.

JOHN CALVIN (1509–1564), PROTESTANT THEOLOGIAN

+++

Light griefs speak out; great griefs are dumb.

LUCIUS ANNAEUS SENECA (3 BCE–AD 65)

+++

I'm learning how to be lonely.

A FRIEND ONE YEAR AFTER HER HUSBAND'S DEATH.

+++

He's everywhere. I talk to him all the time.
I hope they're enjoying him as much up there as I did here.

A WIDOW THE DAY AFTER HER HUSBAND'S DEATH

+++

Sometimes I cry, sometimes I feel numb,
sometimes I actually feel content with his spirit present.

A FRIEND TWO YEARS AFTER HER HUSBAND'S DEATH

I have returned to work, and while I do not have the focus which I once had, I assume I will recover enough to be effective. Some structure, old friends and familiar surroundings are helpful. In time you move to a different place, not because you will it, but because you can't stay where you are. I can't claim any special insight. I'm just doing the best I can.

A WIDOWER TEN WEEKS AFTER LOSING HIS WIFE

+++

Never try to imagine the experience of losing your wife, and do not try to prepare for such an eventuality. No anticipation can alleviate that which strikes when the time comes. But I must and I will trust Him always, though I seem be lost and in the shadow of death.

AN OLD COLLEAGUE, WELL MARRIED FOR FIFTY YEARS

+++

The death of my wife trivializes current experiences – politics, careers, news, sports, and the contemporary scene.

A WIDOWER

+++

'She is in God's hand.' That gains new energy when I think of her as a sword.

A GRIEF OBSERVED, P.50, CLIVE STAPLES LEWIS

I was listening to the conversation of some retired business women, two of whom were part of a worshipping community. The rest did not worship, pray or have any formal religious practice. Three of them were widows. When I asked the widows if they talked to their husbands, they said, "Of course, all the time" Perhaps that's how they prayed.

+++

Why was I so lucky? Where has she gone?
There must be something for which we can find no words,
no frame of reference, no ability to express or even imagine.
Life cannot be just a moment in time, something
between birth and death. Is that really all?

A WIDOWER ONE YEAR AFTER HIS WIFE'S DEATH

+++

Unlike many improvised wedding vows the traditional vows are utterly realistic about death. The couple end their espousals with the phrase, "so long as you both shall live." They pledge themselves to each other "until death do us part." They exchange rings concluding with the words, "so long as we both shall live."

One member of a couple will likely die before the other. To know this makes the couple's life more precious. It also frees the survivor to live as she or he may choose.

Not that survivors forget. How could they? Memories of places, meals, household rituals, conversations, trips, their life together – all these live in the survivor. Two widows told me that they saw their departed husbands. No, they said, they did not imagine them. They saw them. Both husbands seemed happy and content.

Rituals of remembrance such as Jahrzeit in Judaism, the *panikida* in Orthodox churches and visits to the grave for anyone can provide comfort and continuing connection. Earth burial provides a place where the living can remember their dead,

The importance of a burial place cannot be overemphasized. An unmourned death can be a tyrant says Murray Bowen, founder of family systems therapy. From his perspective as a family counselor he concludes that unresolved grief can generate family dissension and dysfunction for generations. He adds that part of a survivor's healing is going to the gravesite of the beloved, speaking to the deceased and listening for whatever voice may come, however it may come.

Love is what is left over
when being in love has burned away,
and this is both an art and a fortunate
accident. Your mother and I had it.

We had roots that grew towards
each other underground,
and when all the pretty blossoms
had fallen from our branches,
we found that we were
one tree, not two.

My Favorite Quotation

My favorite quote is on the opposite page. It's from *Corelli's Mandolin*, written by Louis de Bernieres.

But the roots go even deeper than this quote suggests. Many years after Faith and I were married I came to realize that we had not just married each other. We had married marriage. We had joined a company of women and men who over the centuries have pledged themselves to each other and tried to live that pledge.

By marrying each other Faith and I became more deeply a part of humanity. When we found that pledge hard to keep, the company of the married, including our families, held us together.

So did prayer. In our wedding service the first words we said after our vows were those of the Lord's Prayer. During those painful times when we could hardly speak to each other, we could speak to God and whatever God "said" to us helped to heal us. Our marriage was grounded not only in humanity but in the very ground of our being. And here we are by God's grace sixty-two years later.

The People Who Made This Book Possible

I want first to thank my friend Kathy Page, author of the *Faith Fairchild* detective stories, who urged me to publish my then ragged collection of quotations. She gave me the title for this book, and encouraged me several times when I was ready to bag the project.

Thanks to Betsy Peterson for her good advice and whose collection of quotations, *Voices of Alzheimers*, became the model for this book.

Thanks to the couples who read a draft of this book, and whose responses guided me in shaping its future. They are Elizabeth and Chris Barnett, Lynn and Jason Baskett, Lorna Forbes and Ric Holt, Cori Martin and Hanno Hamlin, Kathy Page and Alan Hein, and Karen and Dan Taylor.

Thanks to my wife who edited several drafts of this book, improved and clarified the text with her suggestions, and without once complaining endured my absences, both physical and mental.

Thanks to the Benedictine monks of Glastonbury Abbey in Hingham MA, whose hospitality gave me a place where I could work with deep focus, restored by their daily services.

Many thanks to Karen Taylor, who gave me good advice through this book's twelve iterations and painstakingly edited the last two. Karen also introduced me to Vicky Sax.

Vicky created the format and layout of this book and prepared it for publication. Her care, creativity, experience and judgement should by now be evident to you.

Thanks to family, friends, former parishioners, colleagues and others whose words I've read or heard and brought to you in this collection.

Thanks, finally, to you, dear reader. I hope you have found here a few insights into the mystery of marriage, and perhaps a few smiles as well.